Dear Santa!

_____

_____

_____

_____

_____

_____

_____

_____

_____

Merry Christmas!

COLOR SANTA

NEW ORNAMENTS

Christmas Ornaments

Tell Santa All Your
Christmas Wishes

Tell Santa All Your
Christmas Wishes

Do your best wrapping paper on this page!

Glue presents everywhere!

My Christmas Wish

FOR THE WORLD

_____

_____

_____

_____

_____

_____

_____

_____

_____

_____

Use lot's of glitter!

SANTA LOVES SNOWFLAKES

TIME FOR
SWEATER DECORATING

Make a silly Christmas Sweater

Don't forget the Glitter

REINDEER TREATS
Glue yummy Reindeer Treats

Tell Santa about you

North Pole

Tell Santa about you

North Pole

_____

_____

_____

_____

_____

_____

_____

_____

_____

_____

Ornament Decorating Time!

Remeber Santa Loves Glitter

Remeber Santa Loves Glitter

Ornament Decorating Time!

Cookie Time!

Cookie Time!

Santa loves gingerbread houses!

Don't forget to glue the candy

MAKE THE
PENGUIN A SCARF

CHRISTMAS COUNTDOWN

DRESS THE DANCING POLAR BEAR

DRESS THE POLAR BEAR

GIFT FOR SANTA CLAUSE

FROM _____

MERRY CHRISTMAS!

Printed in France by Amazon
Brétigny-sur-Orge, FR